REX CHAPMAN

ANTHONY MASON

BARON DAVIS

ALONZO MOURNING

VLADE DIVAC

MUGGSY BOGUES

JAMAL MASHBURN

DAVID WESLEY

BOBBY PHILLS

LARRY JOHNSON

EDDIE JONES

GLEN RICE

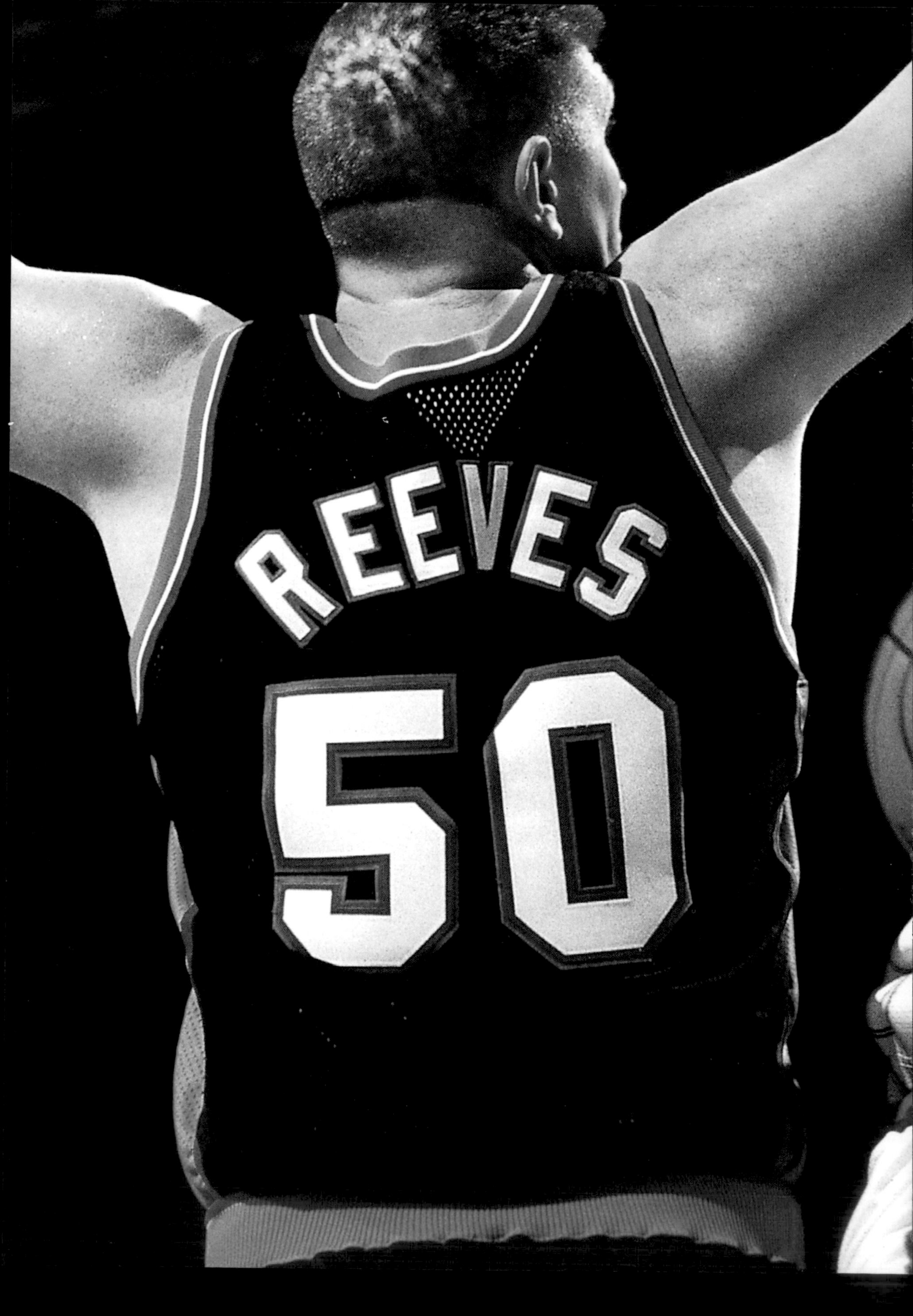
REEVES
50

CREATIVE ✿ EDUCATION

JOHN NICHOLS

Published by Creative Education, 123 South Broad Street, Mankato, MN 56001

Creative Education is an imprint of The Creative Company.

Design and Art Direction by Rita Marshall

Photos by Active Images, Allsport, Rich Kane, NBA Photos

Library of Congress Cataloging-in-Publication Data

Nichols, John, 1966- The history of the Charlotte Hornets / by John Nichols.

p. cm. — (Pro basketball today)   ISBN 1-58341-092-9   1. Charlotte Hornets (Basketball team)—

Juvenile literature. [1. Charlotte Hornets (Basketball team)—History. 2. Basketball—History.] I. Title. II. Series.

GV885.52.C4 N54 2001   796.323′64′0975676—dc21   00-047338

First Edition 9 8 7 6 5 4 3 2 1

THE CITY
OF CHARLOTTE
LIES NEAR THE CATAWBA RIVER

IN SOUTH-CENTRAL NORTH CAROLINA. THE CITY WAS

founded in 1750 and named after Princess Charlotte Sophia, the eventual

bride of King George III of England. During the Revolutionary War, the

citizens of Charlotte wreaked so much havoc upon the English army that

British general Charles Cornwallis likened the city to a hornets' nest.

More than 200 years later, a hornets' nest is still the official emblem

of the city of Charlotte. Its citizens' unconquerable spirit has helped the

city grow into one of the Southeast's most prosperous communities. In

1988, the city was given another cause to get behind: a new franchise in

KELLY TRIPUCKA

the National Basketball Association (NBA). Fittingly, that team was named the Charlotte Hornets.

{THE FIRST YEARS} The Hornets' first season was exciting in many ways and disappointing in others. The team did not have a great deal of talent, as most of the players were either past their prime or were young and inexperienced. Despite their lack of firepower and marquee players, the Hornets were still a huge hit with North Carolina fans. A big reason for the team's popularity in its first season was the play of guards Tyrone "Muggsy" Bogues and Rex Chapman.

The 5-foot-3 and 140-pound Bogues came to the Hornets as an expansion draft pick from the Washington Bullets. By far the smallest player in the league, Bogues had always been overlooked and underestimated as a basketball player. He made up for his short stature with other

BOBBY PHILLS

Guard Rex Chapman's great shooting made him Charlotte's first star.

REX CHAPMAN

attributes, though. Bogues sparked the Hornets' offense by pushing the

ball down the court and hitting open teammates with pinpoint passes. On

defense, his blazing speed, quick hands, and great instincts

gave opposing point guards fits. "Muggsy is our spark

plug," said Hornets forward Kelly Tripucka. "When he

comes in, we all pick up our game a notch."

J.R. Reid and Armon Gilliam combined to snare 17 rebounds a game in **1989–90**.

    The Hornets had selected Chapman, a former

University of Kentucky star, with their first-ever draft pick in 1988. "Rex   **9**

can shoot, he can drive, and he can jump out of the gym," noted head

coach Dick Harter. Unfortunately, the Hornets had few other weapons,

and the team finished with a record of 20–62.

    In an attempt to improve the team's interior defense and offensive

attack, the Hornets added some muscle before the 1989–90 season, draft-

ing 6-foot-9 power forward J.R. Reid from the University of North

J.R. REID

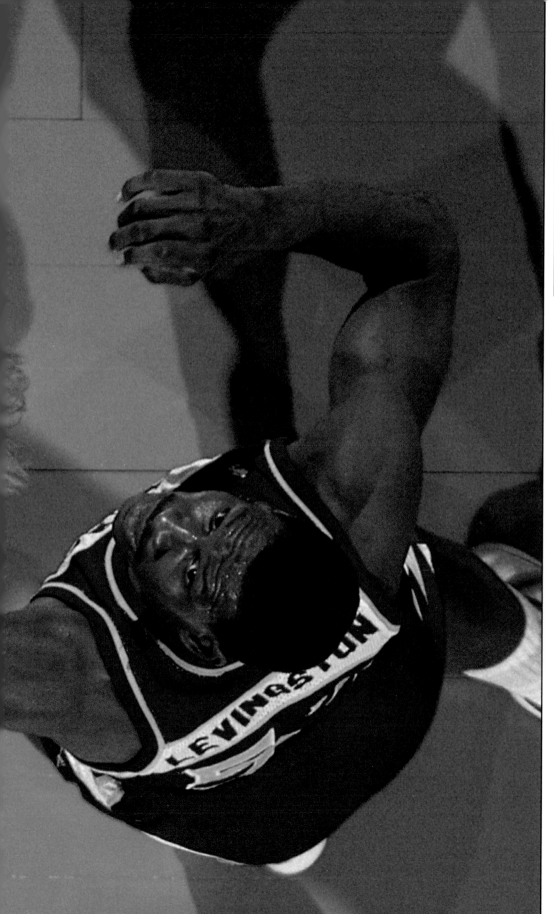

The Hornets were driven in their early years by such hardworking players as Kurt Rambis.

KURT RAMBIS

Carolina and trading for brawny forward Armon Gilliam. The Hornets'

hopes were quickly dashed, however, as the team got off to a miserable

In a
1991–92
game,
Charlotte set
a team record
by beating
Philadelphia
by 52 points.

8–32 start. Harter was then replaced as head coach by assis-

tant Gene Littles.

The new coach tried to jumpstart the team by installing

a fast-break offense, but the young Hornets struggled to

adjust to the new up-tempo style. Unable to boost

Charlotte out of the Eastern Conference cellar, Littles resigned as head

coach after the 1990–91 season.

{JOHNSON AND MOURNING ADD STING} Under new head

coach Allan Bristow, the Hornets' luck began to change. The team raised

its talent level dramatically after striking gold in the NBA Draft two years

in a row with first-round picks Larry Johnson in 1991 and Alonzo

Mourning in 1992.

LARRY JOHNSON

The powerful 6-foot-7 Johnson joined the Hornets after an amazing college career at the University of Nevada-Las Vegas. The 1991 College Player of the Year gave the Hornets their first true superstar, averaging 19

points and 11 rebounds per game his rookie year. This sensational first-year performance earned Johnson the NBA Rookie of the Year award and put Charlotte on the map at last.

The 6-foot-10 and 250-pound Mourning arrived in Charlotte as the second overall pick in the 1992 Draft. The former Georgetown University center boasted a lethal combination of strength and agility, topped off by an intense attitude that made opponents think twice about challenging him. "Most rookies are a little intimidated coming into this league," said Bristow. "'Zo never backs down from anybody."

With Johnson and Mourning anchoring the front line, and Bogues, guard Kendall Gill, and sweet-shooting swingman Dell Curry handling the ball, the Hornets surged into playoff contention in 1992–93. The Hornets finished the season 44–38 and drew the veteran Celtics in the first round of the postseason. Charlotte was a heavy underdog, but the young Hornets were brimming with confidence. "Boston's got all those championships," noted Mourning, "but they didn't win any of them against us."

ALONZO MOURNING

The Celtics cruised to an easy victory in the first game of the series,

but Charlotte then bounced back to win the next two games. In game four,

down 103–102 with three seconds to go, the Hornets worked the ball to

Mourning at the top of the key. Mourning rose up and unleashed a 20-foot

jumper that found the bottom of the net. Bedlam erupted in the Charlotte

Coliseum as the Hornets and their fans celebrated the franchise's first playoff series triumph. Although Charlotte was eliminated by the New York Knicks in the second round, the Hornets and their young stars seemed to be on their way.

{BAD LUCK FOLLOWS THE HORNETS} Thrilled by his young team's rise to prominence, Hornets owner George Shinn rewarded Johnson with a 12-year, $84-million contract extension in 1993—the most lucrative deal in league history. The signing sent shock waves through the NBA, as other

owners questioned Shinn for giving such a large contract to a player entering only his third pro season. "That kind of contract is an enormous gamble," said Phoenix Suns owner Jerry Colangelo.

Colangelo's words rang true during a pregame warm-up early in the 1993–94 season, when Johnson felt a sharp pain shoot from his lower back down his legs. Johnson had suffered a serious back injury that would

MUGGSY BOGUES

force him to miss almost half the season. To make matters worse,

Mourning suffered injuries that sidelined him for several weeks as well.

Determined to carry on without their two stars, the Hornets rallied around Bogues, Curry, and guard Hersey Hawkins to post a respectable 41–41 record. Still, without their talented frontcourt, they came up just short in the race for a playoff spot.

The next season, Johnson and Mourning were back. The big center was at full strength, but Johnson's bad back forced him to change his game. The muscular forward was unable to bull his way to the basket as he had before, and his high-rising leaps were a thing of the past. Johnson made up for it by developing an accurate outside shot, but it was clear he was not the power player he had been. "Larry is still a great player," noted Coach Bristow. "He's just a different kind of player."

VLADE DIVAC

Even with Johnson at less than full strength, the Hornets put

together a strong season. Mourning blossomed into a superstar, averaging

21 points and nearly 10 rebounds per game, while Johnson poured in an

additional 18 points a night. Behind these solid efforts, the Hornets won

50 games for the first time in franchise history. In the playoffs, however,

Michael Jordan and the Chicago Bulls made short work of the Hornets, eliminating them in four games.

{REBUILDING WITH RICE} Before the 1995–96 season, the

Hornets found themselves in a predicament. Mourning was

now in the same position that Johnson had been in two

years before. He had established himself as an All-Star and

wanted to be paid like one. Unable to afford both stars, the

Hornets traded Mourning and two other players to the

Guard Dell Curry netted a team-record 9,839 points in a decade with the Hornets.

Miami Heat for high-scoring forward Glen Rice, point guard Khalid

Reeves, center Matt Geiger, and a first-round draft pick. "It was an

extremely difficult decision," said Bristow. "But we had to do what's best

for the team."

The Hornets struggled after the trade, and a 103–100 loss to

Orlando on the season's last day ended their postseason hopes. After the

season, Bristow was fired and replaced by former Boston Celtics great

DELL CURRY

In his three seasons in Charlotte, versatile scorer Glen Rice averaged 23 points a game.

GLEN RICE

Dave Cowens. To lower their payroll, the Hornets also decided to trade

Johnson. The two-time All-Star was dealt to the New York Knicks for

another muscular forward, Anthony Mason. Charlotte

also acquired 7-foot-1 center Vlade Divac in a trade with

the Los Angeles Lakers.

With Charlotte led by a new coach and a roster of

new players, many fans expected the Hornets to struggle

in 1996–97. Instead, the team started quickly and never looked back. A

major factor in the team's rise was the play of Divac and Mason. The

6-foot-8 and 250-pound Mason showed great versatility, averaging 16

points, 11 rebounds, and nearly 6 assists a game. Divac also proved to be

a solid scorer and was one of the league's top shot blockers.

Still, the brightest star in Charlotte was Rice. The smooth forward

finished third in the NBA in scoring with close to 27 points a game and

Physical forward Anthony Mason was part of a tough front-court in the late **1990s**.

25

ANTHONY MASON

was one of the league's deadliest three-point shooters. Rice and the

Hornets were particularly dangerous playing in front of the hometown

fans at the Charlotte Coliseum—otherwise known as "the Hive." Backed

by its great home-court advantage, Charlotte finished the regular season

with a franchise-best 54–28 record. Unfortunately, the Hornets were hin-

dered by nagging injuries in the playoffs, and the New York Knicks easily swept them in three games in the first round.

The next season, the Hornets traded Muggsy Bogues to Golden State and added free agent guards David Wesley and Bobby Phills. This new backcourt led the Hornets to a 51–31 record and a first-round playoff win over the Atlanta Hawks. But in the second round of the playoffs, the Hornets were eliminated by the powerful Chicago Bulls. "We played hard, but we've still got a ways to go to be a champion," said a disappointed Coach Cowens.

Upon his **1998** arrival, Derrick Coleman became the team's main force in the middle.

{SOLID WITH SILAS} Unrest between NBA players and owners caused a lockout that shortened the regular season to 50 games in 1998–99. When the season finally began, the Hornets featured a revised lineup. The team had added All-Star power forward Derrick Coleman through free agency but had lost Divac and Geiger to other teams. Rice

DERRICK COLEMAN

was sidelined by off-season elbow surgery, and Mason had sustained a

season-ending arm injury during training camp.

Without these players, the Hornets limped to a 4–11

start before Dave Cowens resigned as head coach and was

replaced by assistant coach Paul Silas. Silas had earned a

reputation as a fierce competitor during his NBA playing

days as a forward in the 1960s and '70s, and he quickly

28 conveyed his never-say-die attitude to his team. "Paul told us we could sit

around and lick our wounds, or we could go out and make something of

our season," explained Wesley.

Two days after Silas was hired, the Hornets put together a major

trade that sent Rice, J.R. Reid, and point guard B.J. Armstrong to the Los

Angeles Lakers for swingman Eddie Jones and forward Elden Campbell.

With the addition of this new talent, Charlotte went on a tear, winning

DAVID WESLEY

22 of its last 35 games and barely missing the playoffs.

With the return of a healthy Mason and the addition of talented

rookie point guard Baron Davis, Silas and the Hornets had

high hopes for the 1999–00 season. Sadly, early in the sea-

son, the team was struck by tragedy when a car accident

claimed the life of veteran guard Bobby Phills. The

Hornets honored their fallen friend by playing hard and

finishing the regular season 49–33. But in the playoffs, Charlotte once

again fell—this time to the Philadelphia 76ers.

Following the season, the Hornets made several aggressive moves.

First, they chose rugged forward Jamaal Magloire from the University of

Kentucky with their top pick in the 2000 NBA Draft. Then they traded

Jones and Mason to Miami for power forwards P.J. Brown and Otis

Thorpe and small forward Jamal Mashburn. "Otis and P.J. give us big-time

Ball-hawking swingman Eddie Jones averaged almost three steals a game in **1999–00**.

EDDIE JONES

Guard Baron Davis's explosive scoring ability made him a fan favorite at "the Hive."

BARON DAVIS

Jamal Mashburn combined great inside power and outside shooting.

JAMAL MASHBURN

strength and defensive intensity," said Coach Silas, "and Jamal will give us a consistent scorer and a long-distance threat."

Long-armed forward Elden Campbell patrolled the paint as the team's top shot blocker.

As Charlotte looks to the future, the team and its fans take pride in their past. In a little more than a decade, the franchise has risen from humble expansion roots to become one of the NBA's most competitive organizations. With continued improvement and the backing of the

Charlotte faithful, the Hornets hope to soon swarm over an NBA title.

ELDEN CAMPBELL